This Journal Belongs to:

_____

52 Affirmations for Caregivers of Young Ladies Stuck in the Middle

Copyright

ISBN: 978-1-950649-68-6

Dedication

Without the Father God in Heaven, none of this would be possible. So, I give all praises to you. This book is dedicated to my parents, Katherine Broadous and Kevin Howard. I hope you all are in heaven looking down, thinking, "You did it. Against the odds. You did it!"

My Aunt Dorothy, you mean the world to me and when I felt all alone. I always knew I had you. You showed me what a strong woman looked like and how she should act. I will always be indebted to you.

This journal is inspired by my husband, best friend, and soulmate.

To my M & M's. I do this for you.

Preface:

Preface: Stuck in the middle of not being a dependent child but not yet ready to be an independent adult. According to Eric Erikson, who was a Danish-German-American developmental psychologist and psychoanalyst known for his theory on the psychological development of human beings. He coined the phrase identity crisis. Erickson stated that the stages of development between the age of 12-18 adolescence are very impressionable. At this stage in adolescence, young ladies are trying to figure out who they are and where they belong in this very large world. I wrote this book because I couldn't rely on others, school, social media, and even family to boost my girls' confidence and self-worth. As their mother, it was my job to deposit gems of confidence, self-worth, and positivity into their growing minds. Please use this guide to help build the confidence of our girls and show them that self-confidence starts with how they view themselves.

How to use this book:

This book is a partnership between a caregiver and a young lady.

- Set aside a time when you and your adolescent can have an intimate time of reflection. It will be most beneficial if the time is consistent and free of distractions. At the beginning of the week, read the Affirmation together.

- Next, write the affirmations on a notecard or a piece of paper as reminders throughout the week. * (Mirrors are a great placement) be as creative or simple as you choose for these postcard reminders.

- Then use your journal to write about things that come up when you think of these affirmations. Use your guided journal prompts to guide your reflection. Both caregivers and young ladies will use the journal prompt in separate journals.

- After completing the journal entries, the young lady and caregiver will swap journals.

- Lastly, there is a comments section for positive, non-judgmental comments. Caregivers and young ladies can use this journal to communicate with each other and strengthen their communication.

Affirmations

1. I am more than enough
2. I am powerful
3. I am naturally beautiful
4. I am an original and there is no one else like me
5. I am strong
6. I can make new friends
7. My attitude and opinion are signs of a natural-born leader
8. I learn from my mistakes and my mistakes don't define me
9. I will give my best in everything I do
10. I am smart and talented
11. I can say sorry when I have done wrong
12. I am strong and healthy
13. I do what is right even when no one is looking
14. I have a brilliant and creative mind
15. I can ask for help when I need it
16. I enjoy learning new things
17. I am a good friend
18. I am going to work hard to be my best
19. I am not responsible for other people's actions only my own
20. I am a happy person who has positive energy to give
21. I am a compassionate person
22. My life matters
23. I have people around me who love and care about me
24. I am not alone
25. I am not like everyone else I am a uniquely made, extraordinary individual who has the power to change the world
26. What people say about me doesn't matter as much as how I feel about myself

27. I am a good learner

28. I am respectful, and I deserve respect

29. I am confident

30. When I am mad I can take deep breaths to calm down

31. I am helpful

32. I am a kind person

33. I can control my emotions and my body

34. I am important

35. I am loved

36. I am bold and courageous

37. I am resilient

38. I believe in myself

39. I can do anything I put my mind too

40. I am a hard worker

41. I can work well alone or with friends

42. I can achieve all my goals

43. I am a good reader

44. Learning math isn't always easy but I can do it

45. I am working hard to be the best student

46. I avoid danger, unsafe behavior, and people who will hurt other people because I am a good friend

47. I am a good listener and I listen to learn, understand and get directions

48. I will follow the rules because they are meant to keep me safe and not harm me

49. I can and will always operate as my best self

50. I will do my best every time

51. I am not average and will not conform to stereotypes

52. I am not lazy, too emotional nor weak. I am a young lady who is developing into a strong and mighty woman

Bonus: I will do my best the first time asked

 *Journal*

Weekly Affirmation:

What does this Affirmation mean to you?

_____

_____

Do you agree that this is true about you? And why?

Circle one:		
Strongly agree	*Somewhat agree*	*Not at all agree*

What do you commit to working on this week to assure that you are a reflection of the affirmation that you just spoke?

_____

_____

What are your fears/worries/ troubles/ shortcomings that you are thinking about this week?

_____

_____

How can I help you to have a good week?

_____

_____

_____

_____

Reader's Comment:

Mid -Week Check In?

Reader's Comment:

End of Week Check-in?

Overall, how do you rate your week?

1	2	3	4	5	6	7	8	9	1 0

BAD   GOOD

What worked well?

_____

_____

_____

_____

_____

_____

_____

_____

_____

_____

_____

_____

_____

_____

_____

_____

_____

Rate how you feel about yourself this week?

1	2	3	4	5	6	7	8	9	1 0

Not confident   Super confident

Reader's Comment:

 *Journal*

Weekly Affirmation:

What does this Affirmation mean to you?

_____

_____

Do you agree that this is true about you? And why?

Circle one:		
Strongly agree	*Somewhat agree*	*Not at all agree*

What do you commit to working on this week to assure that you are a reflection of the affirmation that you just spoke?

_____

_____

What are your fears/worries/ troubles/ shortcomings that you are thinking about this week?

_____

_____

How can I help you to have a good week?

_____

_____

_____

_____

Reader's Comment:

Mid -Week Check In?

Reader's Comment:

End of Week Check-in?

Overall, how do you rate your week?

1	2	3	4	5	6	7	8	9	1 0

BAD   GOOD

What worked well?

_____

_____

_____

_____

_____

_____

_____

_____

_____

_____

_____

_____

_____

_____

_____

_____

Rate how you feel about yourself this week?

1	2	3	4	5	6	7	8	9	1 0

Not confident   Super confident

Reader's Comment:

 *Journal*

Weekly Affirmation:

What does this Affirmation mean to you?

_____

_____

Do you agree that this is true about you? And why?

Circle one:		
Strongly agree	_Somewhat agree_	_Not at all agree_

What do you commit to working on this week to assure that you are a reflection of the affirmation that you just spoke?

_____

_____

What are your fears/worries/ troubles/ shortcomings that you are thinking about this week?

_____

_____

How can I help you to have a good week?

_____

_____

_____

_____

Reader's Comment:

Mid -Week Check In?

Reader's Comment:

End of Week Check-in?

Overall, how do you rate your week?

1	2	3	4	5	6	7	8	9	1 0

BAD   GOOD

What worked well?

_____

_____

_____

_____

_____

_____

_____

_____

_____

_____

_____

_____

_____

_____

_____

_____

Rate how you feel about yourself this week?

1	2	3	4	5	6	7	8	9	1 0

Not confident   Super confident

Reader's Comment:

 *Journal*

Weekly Affirmation:

What does this Affirmation mean to you?

_____

_____

Do you agree that this is true about you? And why?

Circle one:		
Strongly agree	*Somewhat agree*	*Not at all agree*

What do you commit to working on this week to assure that you are a reflection of the affirmation that you just spoke?

_____

_____

What are your fears/worries/ troubles/ shortcomings that you are thinking about this week?

_____

_____

How can I help you to have a good week?

_____

_____

_____

_____

Reader's Comment:

Mid -Week Check In?

Reader's Comment:

End of Week Check-in?

Overall, how do you rate your week?

1	2	3	4	5	6	7	8	9	1 0

BAD   GOOD

What worked well?

_____

_____

_____

_____

_____

_____

_____

_____

_____

_____

_____

_____

_____

_____

_____

_____

Rate how you feel about yourself this week?

1	2	3	4	5	6	7	8	9	1 0

Not confident   Super confident

Reader's Comment:

 *Journal*

Weekly Affirmation:

What does this Affirmation mean to you?

_____

_____

Do you agree that this is true about you? And why?

Circle one:		
Strongly agree	*Somewhat agree*	*Not at all agree*

What do you commit to working on this week to assure that you are a reflection of the affirmation that you just spoke?

_____

_____

What are your fears/worries/ troubles/ shortcomings that you are thinking about this week?

_____

_____

How can I help you to have a good week?

_____

_____

_____

_____

Reader's Comment:

Mid -Week Check In?

Reader's Comment:

End of Week Check-in?

Overall, how do you rate your week?

1	2	3	4	5	6	7	8	9	1 0

BAD   GOOD

What worked well?

_____

_____

_____

_____

_____

_____

_____

_____

_____

_____

_____

_____

_____

_____

_____

_____

_____

Rate how you feel about yourself this week?

1	2	3	4	5	6	7	8	9	1 0

Not confident   Super confident

Reader's Comment:

Journal

Weekly Affirmation:

What does this Affirmation mean to you?

_____

_____

Do you agree that this is true about you? And why?

Circle one:		
Strongly agree	*Somewhat agree*	*Not at all agree*

What do you commit to working on this week to assure that you are a reflection of the affirmation that you just spoke?

_____

_____

What are your fears/worries/ troubles/ shortcomings that you are thinking about this week?

_____

_____

How can I help you to have a good week?

_____

_____

_____

_____

Reader's Comment:

Mid -Week Check In?

Reader's Comment:

End of Week Check-in?

Overall, how do you rate your week?

1	2	3	4	5	6	7	8	9	1 0

BAD GOOD

What worked well?

_____

_____

_____

_____

_____

_____

_____

_____

_____

_____

_____

_____

_____

_____

_____

_____

_____

Rate how you feel about yourself this week?

1	2	3	4	5	6	7	8	9	1 0

Not confident Super confident

Reader's Comment:

 *Journal*

Weekly Affirmation:

What does this Affirmation mean to you?

_____

_____

Do you agree that this is true about you? And why?

Circle one:		
Strongly agree	*Somewhat agree*	*Not at all agree*

What do you commit to working on this week to assure that you are a reflection of the affirmation that you just spoke?

_____

_____

What are your fears/worries/ troubles/ shortcomings that you are thinking about this week?

_____

_____

How can I help you to have a good week?

_____

_____

_____

_____

Reader's Comment:

Mid -Week Check In?

Reader's Comment:

End of Week Check-in?

Overall, how do you rate your week?

1	2	3	4	5	6	7	8	9	1 0

BAD   GOOD

What worked well?

_____

_____

_____

_____

_____

_____

_____

_____

_____

_____

_____

_____

_____

_____

_____

Rate how you feel about yourself this week?

1	2	3	4	5	6	7	8	9	1 0

Not confident   Super confident

Reader's Comment:

 *Journal*

Weekly Affirmation:

What does this Affirmation mean to you?

_____

_____

Do you agree that this is true about you? And why?

Circle one:		
Strongly agree	*Somewhat agree*	*Not at all agree*

What do you commit to working on this week to assure that you are a reflection of the affirmation that you just spoke?

_____

_____

What are your fears/worries/ troubles/ shortcomings that you are thinking about this week?

_____

_____

How can I help you to have a good week?

_____

_____

_____

_____

Reader's Comment:

Mid -Week Check In?

Reader's Comment:

End of Week Check-in?

Overall, how do you rate your week?

1	2	3	4	5	6	7	8	9	1 0

BAD   GOOD

What worked well?

_____

_____

_____

_____

_____

_____

_____

_____

_____

_____

_____

_____

_____

_____

_____

_____

_____

_____

Rate how you feel about yourself this week?

1	2	3	4	5	6	7	8	9	1 0

Not confident   Super confident

Reader's Comment:

 **Journal**

Weekly Affirmation:

What does this Affirmation mean to you?

_____

_____

Do you agree that this is true about you? And why?

Circle one:		
Strongly agree	_Somewhat agree_	_Not at all agree_

What do you commit to working on this week to assure that you are a reflection of the affirmation that you just spoke?

_____

_____

What are your fears/worries/ troubles/ shortcomings that you are thinking about this week?

_____

_____

How can I help you to have a good week?

_____

_____

_____

_____

Reader's Comment:

Mid -Week Check In?

Reader's Comment:

# End of Week Check-in?

Overall, how do you rate your week?

1	2	3	4	5	6	7	8	9	1 0

BAD   GOOD

What worked well?

_____

_____

_____

_____

_____

_____

_____

_____

_____

_____

_____

_____

_____

_____

_____

_____

_____

_____

Rate how you feel about yourself this week?

1	2	3	4	5	6	7	8	9	1 0

Not confident   Super confident

Reader's Comment:

 *Journal*

Weekly Affirmation:

What does this Affirmation mean to you?

_____

_____

Do you agree that this is true about you? And why?

Circle one:		
Strongly agree	*Somewhat agree*	*Not at all agree*

What do you commit to working on this week to assure that you are a reflection of the affirmation that you just spoke?

_____

_____

What are your fears/worries/ troubles/ shortcomings that you are thinking about this week?

_____

_____

How can I help you to have a good week?

_____

_____

_____

_____

Reader's Comment:

Mid -Week Check In?

Reader's Comment:

End of Week Check-in?

Overall, how do you rate your week?

1	2	3	4	5	6	7	8	9	1 0

BAD   GOOD

What worked well?

_____

_____

_____

_____

_____

_____

_____

_____

_____

_____

_____

_____

_____

_____

_____

_____

_____

Rate how you feel about yourself this week?

1	2	3	4	5	6	7	8	9	1 0

Not confident   Super confident

Reader's Comment:

 Journal

---

Weekly Affirmation:

What does this Affirmation mean to you?

_____

_____

Do you agree that this is true about you? And why?

Circle one:		
Strongly agree	_Somewhat agree_	_Not at all agree_

What do you commit to working on this week to assure that you are a reflection of the affirmation that you just spoke?

_____

_____

What are your fears/worries/ troubles/ shortcomings that you are thinking about this week?

_____

_____

How can I help you to have a good week?

_____

_____

_____

_____

Reader's Comment:

Mid -Week Check In?

End of Week Check-in?

Overall, how do you rate your week?

1	2	3	4	5	6	7	8	9	1 0

BAD   GOOD

What worked well?

_____

_____

_____

_____

_____

_____

_____

_____

_____

_____

_____

_____

_____

_____

_____

_____

Rate how you feel about yourself this week?

1	2	3	4	5	6	7	8	9	1 0

Not confident   Super confident

Reader's Comment:

 Journal

---

Weekly Affirmation:

What does this Affirmation mean to you?

_____

_____

Do you agree that this is true about you? And why?

Circle one:		
Strongly agree	_Somewhat agree_	_Not at all agree_

What do you commit to working on this week to assure that you are a reflection of the affirmation that you just spoke?

_____

_____

What are your fears/worries/ troubles/ shortcomings that you are thinking about this week?

_____

_____

How can I help you to have a good week?

_____

_____

_____

_____

Reader's Comment:

Mid -Week Check In?

Reader's Comment:

End of Week Check-in?

Overall, how do you rate your week?

1	2	3	4	5	6	7	8	9	1 0

BAD   GOOD

What worked well?

_____

_____

_____

_____

_____

_____

_____

_____

_____

_____

_____

_____

_____

_____

_____

_____

_____

Rate how you feel about yourself this week?

1	2	3	4	5	6	7	8	9	1 0

Not confident   Super confident

Reader's Comment:

 **Journal**

Weekly Affirmation:

What does this Affirmation mean to you?

_____

_____

Do you agree that this is true about you? And why?

Circle one:		
Strongly agree	*Somewhat agree*	*Not at all agree*

What do you commit to working on this week to assure that you are a reflection of the affirmation that you just spoke?

_____

_____

What are your fears/worries/ troubles/ shortcomings that you are thinking about this week?

_____

_____

How can I help you to have a good week?

_____

_____

_____

_____

Reader's Comment:

Mid -Week Check In?

Reader's Comment:

End of Week Check-in?

Overall, how do you rate your week?

| 1 | 2 | 3 | 4 | 5 | 6 | 7 | 8 | 9 | 1 0 |

BAD   GOOD

What worked well?

_____

_____

_____

_____

_____

_____

_____

_____

_____

_____

_____

_____

_____

_____

_____

_____

_____

_____

Rate how you feel about yourself this week?

| 1 | 2 | 3 | 4 | 5 | 6 | 7 | 8 | 9 | 1 0 |

Not confident   Super confident

Reader's Comment:

 *Journal*

> **Weekly Affirmation:**

What does this Affirmation mean to you?

_____

_____

Do you agree that this is true about you? And why?

Circle one:		
Strongly agree	*Somewhat agree*	*Not at all agree*

What do you commit to working on this week to assure that you are a reflection of the affirmation that you just spoke?

_____

_____

What are your fears/worries/ troubles/ shortcomings that you are thinking about this week?

_____

_____

How can I help you to have a good week?

_____

_____

_____

_____

Reader's Comment:

Mid -Week Check In?

Reader's Comment:

End of Week Check-in?

Overall, how do you rate your week?

1	2	3	4	5	6	7	8	9	1 0

BAD   GOOD

What worked well?

_____

_____

_____

_____

_____

_____

_____

_____

_____

_____

_____

_____

_____

_____

_____

_____

Rate how you feel about yourself this week?

1	2	3	4	5	6	7	8	9	1 0

Not confident   Super confident

Reader's Comment:

 **Journal**

Weekly Affirmation:

What does this Affirmation mean to you?

_____

_____

Do you agree that this is true about you? And why?

Circle one:		
Strongly agree	_Somewhat agree_	_Not at all agree_

What do you commit to working on this week to assure that you are a reflection of the affirmation that you just spoke?

_____

_____

What are your fears/worries/ troubles/ shortcomings that you are thinking about this week?

_____

_____

How can I help you to have a good week?

_____

_____

_____

_____

Reader's Comment:

Mid -Week Check In?

Reader's Comment:

End of Week Check-in?

Overall, how do you rate your week?

1	2	3	4	5	6	7	8	9	1 0

BAD   GOOD

What worked well?

_____

_____

_____

_____

_____

_____

_____

_____

_____

_____

_____

_____

_____

_____

_____

Rate how you feel about yourself this week?

1	2	3	4	5	6	7	8	9	1 0

Not confident   Super confident

Reader's Comment:

Journal

Weekly Affirmation:

What does this Affirmation mean to you?

_____

_____

Do you agree that this is true about you? And why?

Circle one:		
Strongly agree	_Somewhat agree_	_Not at all agree_

What do you commit to working on this week to assure that you are a reflection of the affirmation that you just spoke?

_____

_____

What are your fears/worries/ troubles/ shortcomings that you are thinking about this week?

_____

_____

How can I help you to have a good week?

_____

_____

_____

_____

Reader's Comment:

Mid -Week Check In?

Reader's Comment:

End of Week Check-in?

Overall, how do you rate your week?

1	2	3	4	5	6	7	8	9	1 0

BAD   GOOD

What worked well?

_____

_____

_____

_____

_____

_____

_____

_____

_____

_____

_____

_____

_____

_____

_____

_____

Rate how you feel about yourself this week?

1	2	3	4	5	6	7	8	9	1 0

Not confident   Super confident

Reader's Comment:

 *Journal*

Weekly Affirmation:

What does this Affirmation mean to you?

_____

_____

Do you agree that this is true about you? And why?

Circle one:		
Strongly agree	_Somewhat agree_	_Not at all agree_

What do you commit to working on this week to assure that you are a reflection of the affirmation that you just spoke?

_____

_____

What are your fears/worries/ troubles/ shortcomings that you are thinking about this week?

_____

_____

How can I help you to have a good week?

_____

_____

_____

_____

Reader's Comment:

Mid -Week Check In?

Reader's Comment:

End of Week Check-in?

Overall, how do you rate your week?

1	2	3	4	5	6	7	8	9	1 0

BAD   GOOD

What worked well?

_____

_____

_____

_____

_____

_____

_____

_____

_____

_____

_____

_____

_____

_____

_____

_____

_____

Rate how you feel about yourself this week?

1	2	3	4	5	6	7	8	9	1 0

Not confident   Super confident

Reader's Comment:

 *Journal*

> **Weekly Affirmation:**

What does this Affirmation mean to you?

_____

_____

Do you agree that this is true about you? And why?

Circle one:		
Strongly agree	*Somewhat agree*	*Not at all agree*

What do you commit to working on this week to assure that you are a reflection of the affirmation that you just spoke?

_____

_____

What are your fears/worries/ troubles/ shortcomings that you are thinking about this week?

_____

_____

How can I help you to have a good week?

_____

_____

_____

_____

Reader's Comment:

Mid -Week Check In?

Reader's Comment:

# End of Week Check-in?

Overall, how do you rate your week?

1	2	3	4	5	6	7	8	9	1 0

BAD   GOOD

What worked well?

_____

_____

_____

_____

_____

_____

_____

_____

_____

_____

_____

_____

_____

_____

_____

_____

_____

Rate how you feel about yourself this week?

1	2	3	4	5	6	7	8	9	1 0

Not confident   Super confident

Reader's Comment:

 *Journal*

Weekly Affirmation:

What does this Affirmation mean to you?

_____

_____

Do you agree that this is true about you? And why?

Circle one:		
Strongly agree	*Somewhat agree*	*Not at all agree*

What do you commit to working on this week to assure that you are a reflection of the affirmation that you just spoke?

_____

_____

What are your fears/worries/ troubles/ shortcomings that you are thinking about this week?

_____

_____

How can I help you to have a good week?

_____

_____

_____

_____

Reader's Comment:

Mid -Week Check In?

Reader's Comment:

End of Week Check-in?

Overall, how do you rate your week?

1	2	3	4	5	6	7	8	9	1 0

BAD   GOOD

What worked well?

_____

_____

_____

_____

_____

_____

_____

_____

_____

_____

_____

_____

_____

_____

_____

_____

_____

Rate how you feel about yourself this week?

1	2	3	4	5	6	7	8	9	1 0

Not confident   Super confident

Reader's Comment:

 Journal

---

Weekly Affirmation:

What does this Affirmation mean to you?

_____

_____

Do you agree that this is true about you? And why?

Circle one:		
Strongly agree	_Somewhat agree_	_Not at all agree_

What do you commit to working on this week to assure that you are a reflection of the affirmation that you just spoke?

_____

_____

What are your fears/worries/ troubles/ shortcomings that you are thinking about this week?

_____

_____

How can I help you to have a good week?

_____

_____

_____

_____

Reader's Comment:

Mid -Week Check In?

Reader's Comment:

_____

_____

_____

_____

_____

_____

_____

_____

_____

_____

_____

_____

_____

_____

_____

_____

_____

_____

_____

_____

_____

_____

_____

_____

_____

_____

_____

_____

_____

End of Week Check-in?

Overall, how do you rate your week?

1	2	3	4	5	6	7	8	9	1 0

BAD   GOOD

What worked well?

_____

_____

_____

_____

_____

_____

_____

_____

_____

_____

_____

_____

_____

_____

_____

_____

Rate how you feel about yourself this week?

1	2	3	4	5	6	7	8	9	1 0

Not confident   Super confident

Reader's Comment:

 *Journal*

Weekly Affirmation:

What does this Affirmation mean to you?

_____

_____

Do you agree that this is true about you? And why?

Circle one:		
Strongly agree	*Somewhat agree*	*Not at all agree*

What do you commit to working on this week to assure that you are a reflection of the affirmation that you just spoke?

_____

_____

What are your fears/worries/ troubles/ shortcomings that you are thinking about this week?

_____

_____

How can I help you to have a good week?

_____

_____

_____

_____

Reader's Comment:

Mid -Week Check In?

Reader's Comment:

_____

_____

_____

_____

_____

_____

_____

_____

_____

_____

_____

_____

_____

_____

_____

_____

_____

_____

_____

_____

_____

_____

_____

_____

_____

_____

End of Week Check-in?

Overall, how do you rate your week?

1	2	3	4	5	6	7	8	9	1 0

BAD　　　　　　　　　　　　　　　　　　　　　　　　　　　　　GOOD

What worked well?

_____

_____

_____

_____

_____

_____

_____

_____

_____

_____

_____

_____

_____

_____

_____

_____

_____

Rate how you feel about yourself this week?

1	2	3	4	5	6	7	8	9	1 0

Not confident　　　　　　　　　　　　　　　　　　　　Super confident

Reader's Comment:

 **Journal**

Weekly Affirmation:

What does this Affirmation mean to you?

_____

_____

Do you agree that this is true about you? And why?

Circle one:		
Strongly agree	_Somewhat agree_	_Not at all agree_

What do you commit to working on this week to assure that you are a reflection of the affirmation that you just spoke?

_____

_____

What are your fears/worries/ troubles/ shortcomings that you are thinking about this week?

_____

_____

How can I help you to have a good week?

_____

_____

_____

_____

Reader's Comment:

Mid -Week Check In?

Reader's Comment:

_____
_____
_____
_____
_____
_____
_____
_____
_____
_____
_____
_____
_____
_____
_____
_____
_____
_____
_____
_____
_____
_____
_____
_____
_____
_____
_____

End of Week Check-in?

Overall, how do you rate your week?

1	2	3	4	5	6	7	8	9	1 0

BAD   GOOD

What worked well?

_____

_____

_____

_____

_____

_____

_____

_____

_____

_____

_____

_____

_____

_____

_____

Rate how you feel about yourself this week?

1	2	3	4	5	6	7	8	9	1 0

Not confident   Super confident

Reader's Comment:

 *Journal*

Weekly Affirmation:

What does this Affirmation mean to you?

_____

_____

Do you agree that this is true about you? And why?

Circle one:		
Strongly agree	*Somewhat agree*	*Not at all agree*

What do you commit to working on this week to assure that you are a reflection of the affirmation that you just spoke?

_____

_____

What are your fears/worries/ troubles/ shortcomings that you are thinking about this week?

_____

_____

How can I help you to have a good week?

_____

_____

_____

_____

Reader's Comment:

Mid -Week Check In?

Reader's Comment:

_____
_____
_____
_____
_____
_____
_____
_____
_____
_____
_____
_____
_____
_____
_____
_____
_____
_____
_____
_____
_____
_____
_____
_____
_____
_____

End of Week Check-in?

Overall, how do you rate your week?

1	2	3	4	5	6	7	8	9	1 0

BAD   GOOD

What worked well?

_____

_____

_____

_____

_____

_____

_____

_____

_____

_____

_____

_____

_____

_____

_____

_____

_____

Rate how you feel about yourself this week?

1	2	3	4	5	6	7	8	9	1 0

Not confident   Super confident

Reader's Comment:

 **Journal**

Weekly Affirmation:

What does this Affirmation mean to you?

_____

_____

Do you agree that this is true about you? And why?

Circle one:		
Strongly agree	*Somewhat agree*	*Not at all agree*

What do you commit to working on this week to assure that you are a reflection of the affirmation that you just spoke?

_____

_____

What are your fears/worries/ troubles/ shortcomings that you are thinking about this week?

_____

_____

How can I help you to have a good week?

_____

_____

_____

_____

Reader's Comment:

Mid -Week Check In?

Reader's Comment:

End of Week Check-in?

Overall, how do you rate your week?

1	2	3	4	5	6	7	8	9	1 0

BAD   GOOD

What worked well?

_____

_____

_____

_____

_____

_____

_____

_____

_____

_____

_____

_____

_____

_____

_____

_____

Rate how you feel about yourself this week?

1	2	3	4	5	6	7	8	9	1 0

Not confident   Super confident

Reader's Comment:

 *Journal*

Weekly Affirmation:

What does this Affirmation mean to you?

_____

_____

Do you agree that this is true about you? And why?

Circle one:

Strongly agree   *Somewhat agree*   *Not at all agree*

What do you commit to working on this week to assure that you are a reflection of the affirmation that you just spoke?

_____

_____

What are your fears/worries/ troubles/ shortcomings that you are thinking about this week?

_____

_____

How can I help you to have a good week?

_____

_____

_____

_____

Reader's Comment:

Mid -Week Check In?

Reader's Comment:

 *End of Week Check-in?*

Overall, how do you rate your week?

1	2	3	4	5	6	7	8	9	1 0

BAD   GOOD

What worked well?

_____

_____

_____

_____

_____

_____

_____

_____

_____

_____

_____

_____

_____

_____

_____

_____

_____

_____

Rate how you feel about yourself this week?

1	2	3	4	5	6	7	8	9	1 0

Not confident   Super confident

Reader's Comment:

Journal

> **Weekly Affirmation:**

What does this Affirmation mean to you?

_____

_____

Do you agree that this is true about you? And why?

Circle one:		
Strongly agree	_Somewhat agree_	_Not at all agree_

What do you commit to working on this week to assure that you are a reflection of the affirmation that you just spoke?

_____

_____

What are your fears/worries/ troubles/ shortcomings that you are thinking about this week?

_____

_____

How can I help you to have a good week?

_____

_____

_____

_____

Reader's Comment:

Mid -Week Check In?

Reader's Comment:

End of Week Check-in?

Overall, how do you rate your week?

1	2	3	4	5	6	7	8	9	1 0

BAD   GOOD

What worked well?

_____

_____

_____

_____

_____

_____

_____

_____

_____

_____

_____

_____

_____

_____

_____

_____

_____

_____

Rate how you feel about yourself this week?

1	2	3	4	5	6	7	8	9	1 0

Not confident   Super confident

Reader's Comment:

Letter to my Caregiver:

Thank you for your purchase. This book aims to strengthen your child's self-confidence and reduce anxiety and depression among adolescents. I pray that this affirmation and guided journal will enhance your relationship with your child. This guided journal will also increase your child's writing skills and show them a very productive way to handle their feelings and thoughts by journaling and talking to a trusted adult. One of the biggest hurdles children and adults have is, expressing themselves. Writing in this journal allows them to say how they feel without fear of your immediate reaction. So, choose your words wisely and show compassion. Being a tweener/teenager is not easy; please handle these written expressions with care.

With Love,
Alisha Kelley LCSW

Made in United States
Troutdale, OR
09/11/2023

12821951R00052